HOME SCHOOL DAILY PLANNER

YEAR:_____

HOME SCHOOL DAILY PLANNER

Copyright © 2003 by Kimberley Nash
Published by RESURRECTION RESOURCES LLC
Woodbury, Minnesota 55129
USA
www.thefathersbooks.com

ISBN Number: 0-9653723-2-4

Scripture taken from THE SCRIPTURES, © 1998 by the Institute for Scripture Research (Pty) Ltd. Used by permission.

Protected by International copyright treaties and United States copyright laws.
All rights reserved. No portion of this book may be copied or reproduced in any form.
Offenders will be prosecuted to the full extent of the law.

Printed in the United States of America.

A PRIVILEGE TO PLAN

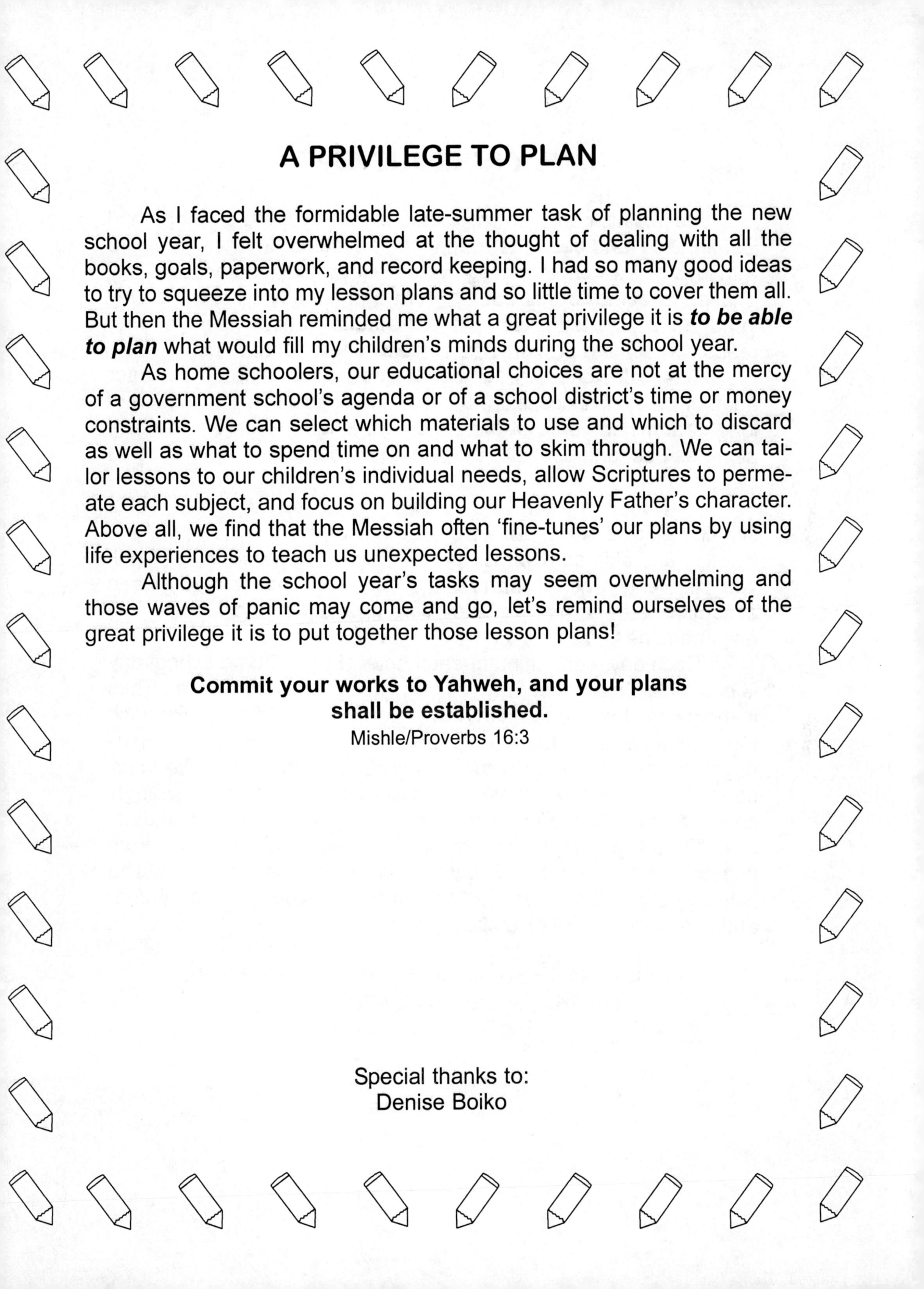

As I faced the formidable late-summer task of planning the new school year, I felt overwhelmed at the thought of dealing with all the books, goals, paperwork, and record keeping. I had so many good ideas to try to squeeze into my lesson plans and so little time to cover them all. But then the Messiah reminded me what a great privilege it is ***to be able to plan*** what would fill my children's minds during the school year.

As home schoolers, our educational choices are not at the mercy of a government school's agenda or of a school district's time or money constraints. We can select which materials to use and which to discard as well as what to spend time on and what to skim through. We can tailor lessons to our children's individual needs, allow Scriptures to permeate each subject, and focus on building our Heavenly Father's character. Above all, we find that the Messiah often 'fine-tunes' our plans by using life experiences to teach us unexpected lessons.

Although the school year's tasks may seem overwhelming and those waves of panic may come and go, let's remind ourselves of the great privilege it is to put together those lesson plans!

Commit your works to Yahweh, and your plans shall be established.
Mishle/Proverbs 16:3

Special thanks to:
Denise Boiko

MY PRECIOUS GIFT

He laid his pencil down, leaned further over the paper he had just finished, and began to read it one final time. My heart swelled with love as I watched him intent on the task. How many years had it taken to come to this point? From a small boy who could only 'read' a story by looking at the pictures, to now: a teenager who reads, writes, and proof-reads his papers without my help!

The milestones in life don't always occur one right after another in rapid succession. Most, if not all, are the culmination of long determined years of alternately working hard or just trudging along as best one can. But they do finally come and the fruit is so sweet!

As I watch my son who no longer wiggles and giggles, but is still and quiet, I see many milestones along the way. They fill me with joy and also sorrow. Joy that we've done a good thing; thank you Heavenly Father! Sorrow that so much has already been accomplished and many of the years of struggle and fun are now only memories.

Each day, each minute, each hour of each home school day is precious. When past they will be joyful, sorrowful, or both. Thus in the years I have left with my son, I continue to plan to make each moment a beautiful memory. Though I had a career before marriage and motherhood, I knew I would always stay home after marriage. Though I could have chosen other alternatives, I willingly chose home school. And I have never regretted a day of that decision. From my decision and the glorious light shining down from heaven, I can share in words what I have received in return. The blessing of a child is two-fold: that in the life you gave to him/her and in the life he/she gives back to you!

Look, children are an inheritance from Yahweh;
The fruit of the womb is the reward.
Tehillim/Psalm 127:3

Special thanks to:
Kimberley Nash

**FOR THIS PRECIOUS STUDENT
I PRAY THIS YEAR...**

CHANGING THE WORLD FROM MY BASEMENT

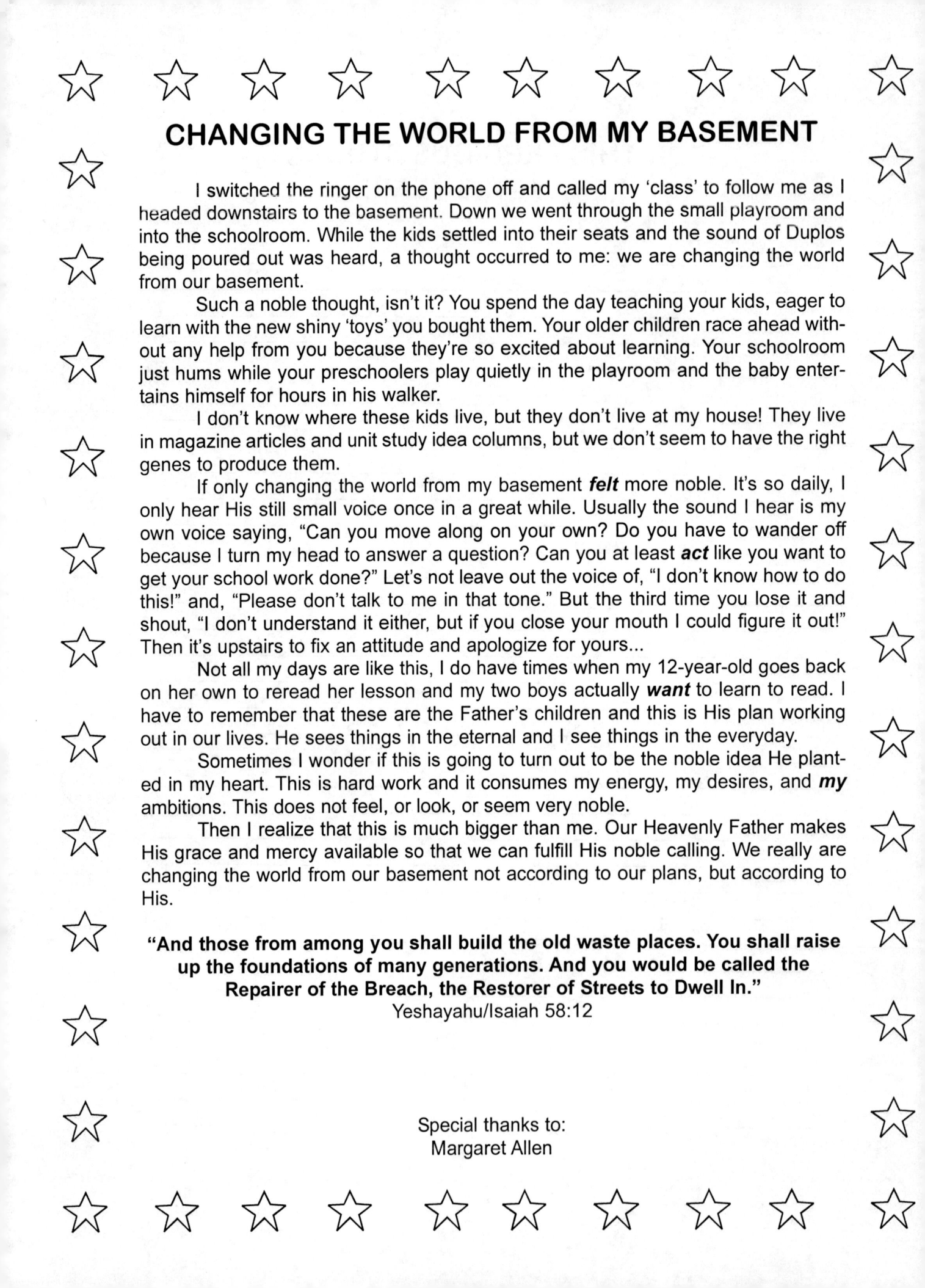

I switched the ringer on the phone off and called my 'class' to follow me as I headed downstairs to the basement. Down we went through the small playroom and into the schoolroom. While the kids settled into their seats and the sound of Duplos being poured out was heard, a thought occurred to me: we are changing the world from our basement.

Such a noble thought, isn't it? You spend the day teaching your kids, eager to learn with the new shiny 'toys' you bought them. Your older children race ahead without any help from you because they're so excited about learning. Your schoolroom just hums while your preschoolers play quietly in the playroom and the baby entertains himself for hours in his walker.

I don't know where these kids live, but they don't live at my house! They live in magazine articles and unit study idea columns, but we don't seem to have the right genes to produce them.

If only changing the world from my basement **felt** more noble. It's so daily, I only hear His still small voice once in a great while. Usually the sound I hear is my own voice saying, "Can you move along on your own? Do you have to wander off because I turn my head to answer a question? Can you at least **act** like you want to get your school work done?" Let's not leave out the voice of, "I don't know how to do this!" and, "Please don't talk to me in that tone." But the third time you lose it and shout, "I don't understand it either, but if you close your mouth I could figure it out!" Then it's upstairs to fix an attitude and apologize for yours...

Not all my days are like this, I do have times when my 12-year-old goes back on her own to reread her lesson and my two boys actually **want** to learn to read. I have to remember that these are the Father's children and this is His plan working out in our lives. He sees things in the eternal and I see things in the everyday.

Sometimes I wonder if this is going to turn out to be the noble idea He planted in my heart. This is hard work and it consumes my energy, my desires, and **my** ambitions. This does not feel, or look, or seem very noble.

Then I realize that this is much bigger than me. Our Heavenly Father makes His grace and mercy available so that we can fulfill His noble calling. We really are changing the world from our basement not according to our plans, but according to His.

"And those from among you shall build the old waste places. You shall raise up the foundations of many generations. And you would be called the Repairer of the Breach, the Restorer of Streets to Dwell In."
Yeshayahu/Isaiah 58:12

Special thanks to:
Margaret Allen

DAILY ATTENDANCE/HOURS

LEGEND

X = PRESENT
O = ABSENT
+ = HOLIDAY

	WEEK 1					WEEK 2					WEEK 3					WEEK 4					WEEK 5					TOTALS
	M	T	W	T	F	M	T	W	T	F	M	T	W	T	F	M	T	W	T	F	M	T	W	T	F	
SEPTEMBER																										
OCTOBER																										
NOVEMBER																										
DECEMBER																										
JANUARY																										
FEBRUARY																										
MARCH																										
APRIL																										
MAY																										
JUNE																										
JULY																										
AUGUST																										
TOTALS																										

NOTES

FIELD TRIPS

DATE	PLACE

SING A SONG OF JOY!

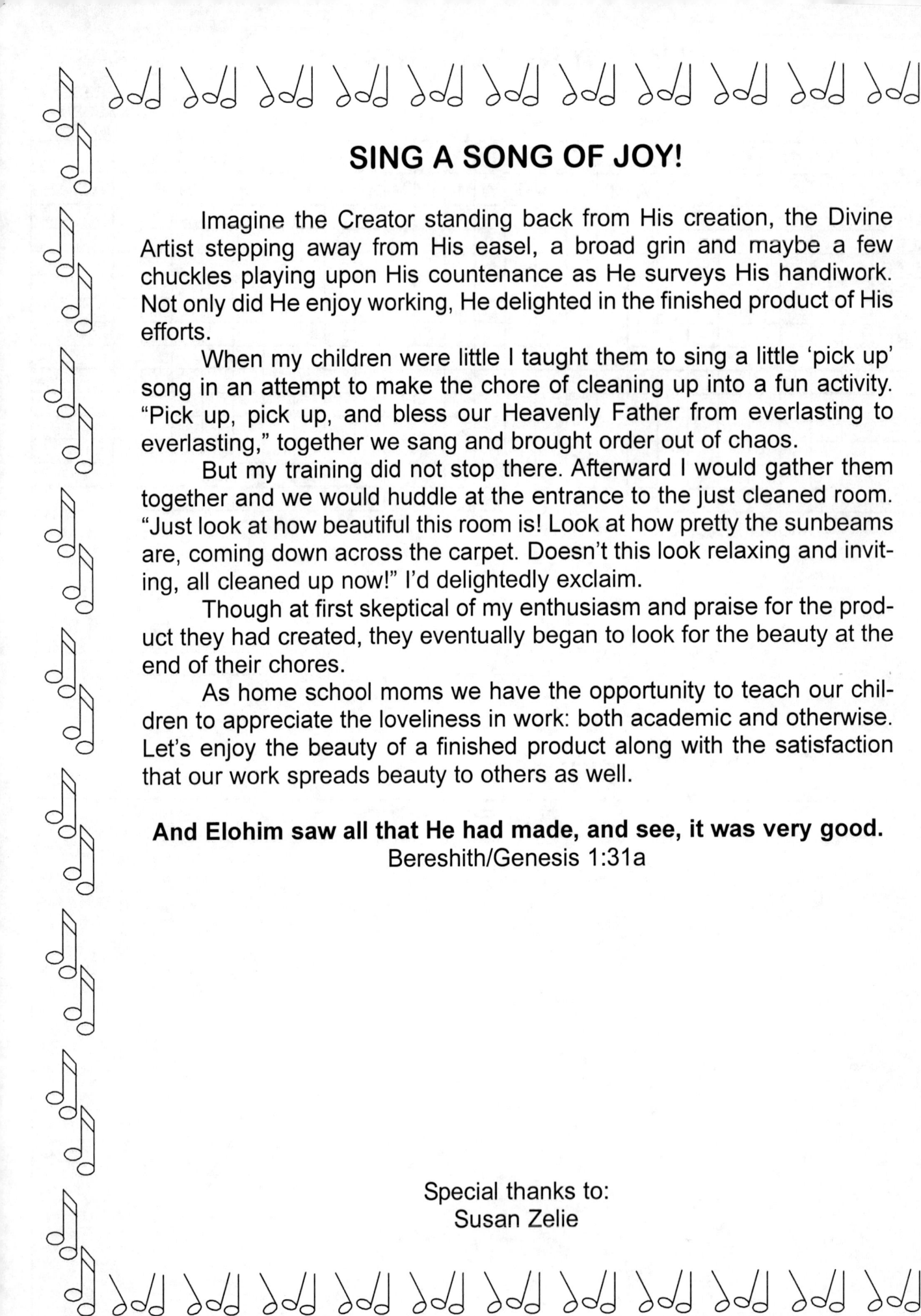

Imagine the Creator standing back from His creation, the Divine Artist stepping away from His easel, a broad grin and maybe a few chuckles playing upon His countenance as He surveys His handiwork. Not only did He enjoy working, He delighted in the finished product of His efforts.

When my children were little I taught them to sing a little 'pick up' song in an attempt to make the chore of cleaning up into a fun activity. "Pick up, pick up, and bless our Heavenly Father from everlasting to everlasting," together we sang and brought order out of chaos.

But my training did not stop there. Afterward I would gather them together and we would huddle at the entrance to the just cleaned room. "Just look at how beautiful this room is! Look at how pretty the sunbeams are, coming down across the carpet. Doesn't this look relaxing and inviting, all cleaned up now!" I'd delightedly exclaim.

Though at first skeptical of my enthusiasm and praise for the product they had created, they eventually began to look for the beauty at the end of their chores.

As home school moms we have the opportunity to teach our children to appreciate the loveliness in work: both academic and otherwise. Let's enjoy the beauty of a finished product along with the satisfaction that our work spreads beauty to others as well.

And Elohim saw all that He had made, and see, it was very good.
Bereshith/Genesis 1:31a

Special thanks to:
Susan Zelie

CHORES CHART

CHORE	M	T	W	T	F
Make bed					
Brush teeth					
Bath					

TIPS

1. Each chore should match your student's age abilities.
2. Be persistent. Have your student do the same chores for the whole school year.
3. Play happy and upbeat music during chores to help keep things moving.
4. Check your student's work.
5. Doing a chore well is learned in a process; don't expect or demand instant mastery.
6. Help your student improve assigned chores at least once a month, until you are satisfied with the mastery level.
7. Do chores at the same time every day.
8. Schedule at least 30 minutes every day for household cleaning chores.
9. Thank your student for a job well done.
10. Visit our web site for more tips and helpful information at: www.thefathersbooks.com

OUR FAMILY RULES

1.	Say thank you and please.
2.	Don't interrupt when someone is speaking.
3.	
4.	
5.	
6.	
7.	
8.	
9.	
10.	
11.	
12.	
13.	
14.	
15.	
16.	
17.	
18.	
19.	
20.	

DAILY SCHEDULE-_____
STUDENT

TIME | SUBJECT

TIME	Monday	Tuesday	Wednesday	Thursday	Friday

SINGING HIS WORD FROM MY HEART!

"For unto....For unto...."My five-year-old daughter was unable to remember the next few words (you is born this day). "Try again, honey," I coached, feeling a panic inside. I wanted to begin hiding Yahweh's word in her heart by including scripture memorization in our curriculum. However, her mind didn't seem to be able to memorize verses, even though I knew her peers could. I wondered what was wrong? Maybe I could try something different. I prayed and prepared every method of teaching I could devise. I broke the verses into small parts, made visual aids, designed games, composed chants, created cheers, and dreamed up a myriad of kinesthetic, visual, and audio experiences. Still nothing clicked.

Then one day as I was singing a worship song that was taken directly from scripture, an idea dawned on me. Perhaps Heidi could learn the verses if we sang them? Frantically, I took the first line of the tune to "The B-I-B-L-E" and applied it to Luke 2:11. "For unto....For unto...." It fit! The next line needed 3 extra notes squeezed in, but it would work: "today in the city of Dawid/David." With excitement I sang the whole verse for Heidi, then encouraged her to sing each phrase after me. She could do it! Victory! My child could memorize after all!

After that my music books with children's songs became well-used as scriptures were matched to melodies such as "Give Me Oil in My Lamp" and "This Little Light of Mine." My gratitude to Yaweh flooded over me each time she mastered another "musical verse" during the next year. Even longer passages, like the 23rd Tehillim/Psalm, were "hidden" in her young heart. But, of course, I wondered if she would always have to sing in order to memorize anything? Occasionally I would try to get her to recite a phrase in a speaking voice, and finally at age 8 she was able to memorize passages without adding a tune. I am so thankful for Yahweh's giving me perseverance back then....and now my heart is thrilled when I hear her nineteen-year-old voice singing a song about her Elohim and speaking about His Word with adoration.

Let the Word of Messiah dwell in you richly, teaching and admonishing one another in all wisdom, singing with pleasure in your hearts to the Master in psalms and songs of praise and spiritual songs.
Colossians 3:16

Special thanks to:
Connie Schondelmeyer

MONTHLY SCRIPTURE MEMORY LOG

1. Scripture:_____**Completion date:**_____
Text:_____
_____

2. Scripture:_____**Completion date:**_____
Text:_____
_____

3. Scripture:_____**Completion date:**_____
Text:_____
_____

4. Scripture:_____**Completion date:**_____
Text:_____
_____

5. Scripture:_____**Completion date:**_____
Text:_____
_____

6. Scripture:_____**Completion date:**_____
Text:_____
_____

7. Scripture:_____**Completion date:**_____
Text:_____
_____

8. Scripture:_____**Completion date:**_____
Text:_____
_____

9. Scripture:_____**Completion date:**_____
Text:_____
_____

10. Scripture:_____**Completion date:**_____
Text:_____
_____

WEEKLY LUNCH/DINNER MENU

SUNDAY	MONDAY	TUESDAY	WEDNESDAY	THURSDAY	FRIDAY	SATURDAY

This page reproducible for purchaser's use for one school year only, not for any other purpose nor for distribution to any other person, group, or organization.

A SISTER IS A FRIEND FOREVER

I'll never forget the day my two oldest daughters came home from swimming lessons giggling. They had been in this class for several weeks before the other swimmers realized they were sisters. One girl boldly questioned, "How can you be such good friends if you're sisters?" You see it was evident to the others that they were indeed friends, but not that they were also sisters.

How sad to think that in our world it is so unnatural for sisters to be friends. In the world it is considered normal for siblings to quarrel, to be competitive, to be rude to one another, to criticize each other, and to each have her own distinct friends. Thus it *is* astonishing to find sisters who truly enjoy each other's company, who ask each other for advice, who are kind, considerate, and polite to one another.

I am so thankful that home school has provided the opportunity for my children to study, work, and play together every single day. They have become best friends for life. And hopefully this friendship will be a lighthouse to the world so that they will know we are born-again believers by the love that is shown in and through our family.

A renewed command I give to you, that you love one another, as I have loved you, that you also love one another. By this shall all know that you are My taught ones, if you have love for one another.
Yohanan/John 13:34-35

Special thanks to:
Kim Ooms

ACTIVITY CHART

ACTIVITY	M	T	W	T	F

NOTES

CHARACTER DEVELOPMENT

	TRAIT	CONSISTENT EVIDENCE
1.	Kindness	
2.		
3.		
4.		
5.		
6.		
7.		
8.		
9.		
10.		

CURRICULA LOG REPORT

STUDENT:_____

GRADE:_____

1. Subject:_____
Book title:_____
Publisher:_____
Grade level:_____   Pages covered:_____

2. Subject:_____
Book title:_____
Publisher:_____
Grade level:_____   Pages covered:_____

3. Subject:_____
Book title:_____
Publisher:_____
Grade level:_____   Pages covered:_____

4. Subject:_____
Book title:_____
Publisher:_____
Grade level:_____   Pages covered:_____

5. Subject:_____
Book title:_____
Publisher:_____
Grade level:_____   Pages covered:_____

6. Subject:_____
Book title:_____
Publisher:_____
Grade level:_____   Pages covered:_____

7. Subject:_____
Book title:_____
Publisher:_____
Grade level:_____   Pages covered:_____

8. Subject:_____
Book title:_____
Publisher:_____
Grade level:_____   Pages covered:_____

9. Subject:_____
Book title:_____
Publisher:_____
Grade level:_____   Pages covered:_____

10. Subject:_____
Book title:_____
Publisher:_____
Grade level:_____   Pages covered:_____

PROBLEMS, PROBLEMS, PROBLEMS

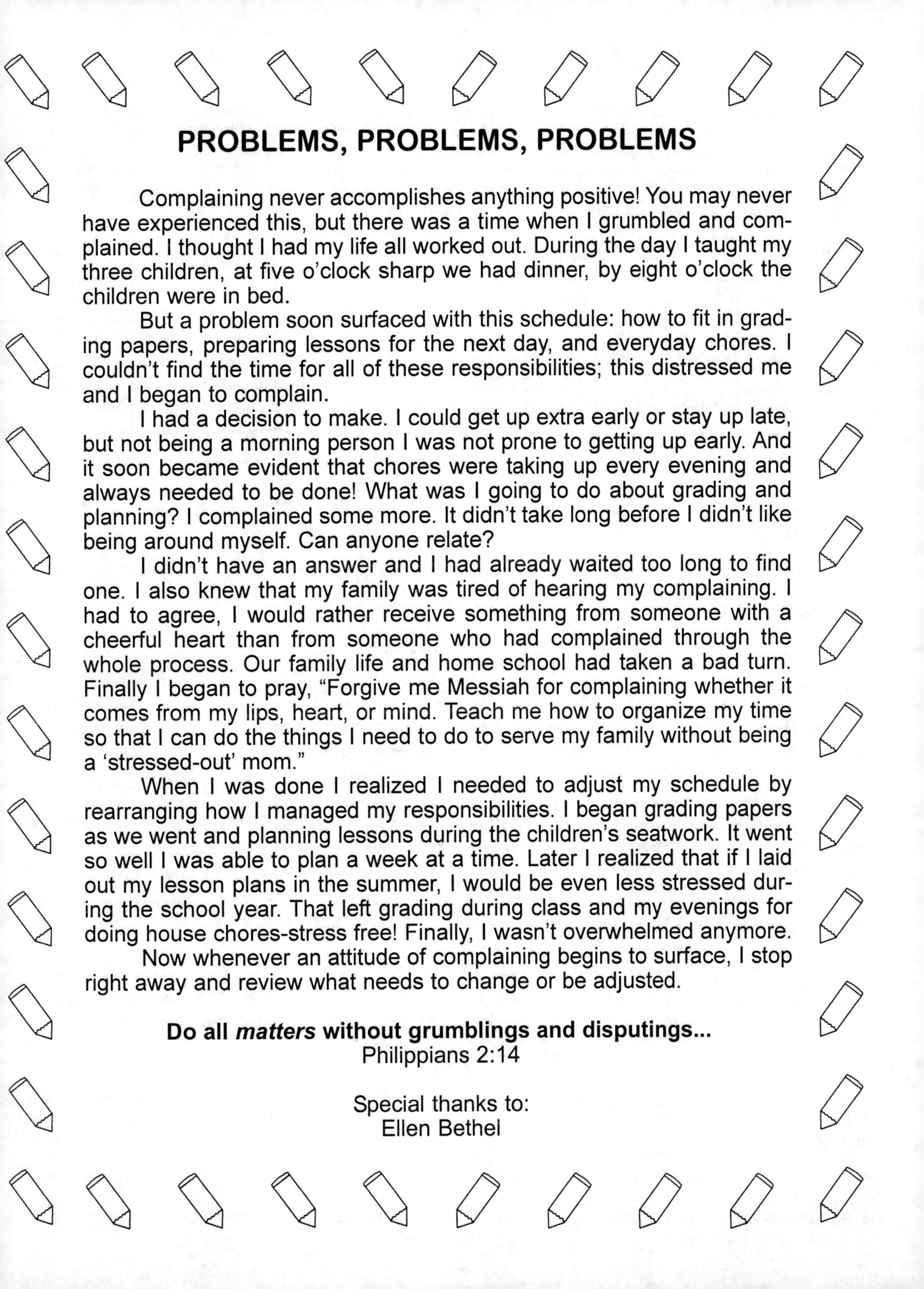

Complaining never accomplishes anything positive! You may never have experienced this, but there was a time when I grumbled and complained. I thought I had my life all worked out. During the day I taught my three children, at five o'clock sharp we had dinner, by eight o'clock the children were in bed.

But a problem soon surfaced with this schedule: how to fit in grading papers, preparing lessons for the next day, and everyday chores. I couldn't find the time for all of these responsibilities; this distressed me and I began to complain.

I had a decision to make. I could get up extra early or stay up late, but not being a morning person I was not prone to getting up early. And it soon became evident that chores were taking up every evening and always needed to be done! What was I going to do about grading and planning? I complained some more. It didn't take long before I didn't like being around myself. Can anyone relate?

I didn't have an answer and I had already waited too long to find one. I also knew that my family was tired of hearing my complaining. I had to agree, I would rather receive something from someone with a cheerful heart than from someone who had complained through the whole process. Our family life and home school had taken a bad turn. Finally I began to pray, "Forgive me Messiah for complaining whether it comes from my lips, heart, or mind. Teach me how to organize my time so that I can do the things I need to do to serve my family without being a 'stressed-out' mom."

When I was done I realized I needed to adjust my schedule by rearranging how I managed my responsibilities. I began grading papers as we went and planning lessons during the children's seatwork. It went so well I was able to plan a week at a time. Later I realized that if I laid out my lesson plans in the summer, I would be even less stressed during the school year. That left grading during class and my evenings for doing house chores-stress free! Finally, I wasn't overwhelmed anymore.

Now whenever an attitude of complaining begins to surface, I stop right away and review what needs to change or be adjusted.

Do all *matters* without grumblings and disputings...
Philippians 2:14

Special thanks to:
Ellen Bethel

SETTING UP THE GRADING CHART

Setting up a daily grading chart is easy! To be successful, however, you must first decide what **subjects** will be taught to your student. Then determine what **type of work** will be graded within each subject: lessons, tests, quizzes, written papers, or other items. Next, list each subject in the **DAILY GRADES** charts making sure to identify each type of work that will be graded within that subject before listing the next subject. Leave enough room between each type of work to be able to record all of the semester's grades without bumping into the next item. For example, suppose that your student will take a science course that will contain lessons, quizzes, and tests. A good spacing scheme might look as follows:

SUBJECT																
Science																
Lessons	B 85	A- 92	A 95	C 75	A 95	B- 82										
Quizzes	B- 82	A 95	A 95	B 85												
Tests	A+ 100	A 95	B 85													
Math																

CALCULATING AND RECORDING GRADES

The following instructions contain three sections. Read each one carefully and review the examples until you understand them.

SECTION A explains how to grade your student's work for each day and record those grades in the **DAILY GRADES** chart.
SECTION B explains how to tally the daily grades for each subject at the end of a semester and calculate an overall grade.
SECTION C explains how to use the two different report cards included in this daily planner.

SECTION A

To determine a grade for each piece of daily work for your student, use **one** of the following methods:

1. For lessons, tests, and quizzes with questions that are fill in the blank, true/false, problem solving in nature, or require short essays, use one of the following two methods (a or b) to determine each grade.

a. Tally the number of correct responses and divide that tally by the total number of responses required. Then multiply the quotient by 100%. Next, refer to **TABLE 1** on the next page to assign a grade. Write both the percentage and grade on your student's paper and in the **DAILY GRADES** charts as illustrated above. **Note:** Fill in the blank, true/false, problem solving, and short essay questions are graded either correct or incorrect in this method.

Example:
-A lesson, quiz, or test has some combination of 67 fill in the blank, true/false, problem solving, or essay questions. Your student completes 64 correctly. Your student's grade is calculated as follows: (64/67) x 100% = **95.5%**   Grade = A

b. Tally the correct score (points) and divide that tally by the total score (points). Then multiply the quotient by 100%. Next, refer to **TABLE 1** to assign a grade. Write the percentage and grade on your student's paper and in the **DAILY GRADES** charts. **Note:** Fill in the blank, true/false, and problem solving questions are graded either correct or incorrect in this method also, but each correct answer is assigned a predetermined score (points). Short essay responses are graded on content plus amount, proper and logical organization, and correct grammar, then assigned a portion of a predetermined score (points).

Example:
-A lesson, quiz, or test has some combination of fill in the blank, true/false, problem solving, or essay questions. A total score of 96 points for the total number of questions is given. The student earns 78 points. The student's grade is calculated as follows: (78/96) x 100% = **81.3%**   Grade = B-

2. For all other types of written papers in our curricula, use the grading instructions and grading charts we provide.

3. For subjective subjects like a foreign language, art, or cooking, base your student's grade on effort, execution, accuracy, neatness, clarity, tastiness, etc.

SECTION B
USE THE GRADE TALLYING CHARTS ON THE FOLLOWING PAGES IN CONJUNCTION WITH THIS SECTION.

1. To determine a **SEMESTER GRADE**, begin by using **Formula 1** (below) to calculate a percentage. Then decide on a grade weight for each type of work. **Note:** The grade weight is how much each type of work will contribute to the final grade. Grade weight must be determined by you. It is sometimes difficult to decide and should be prayed over. However, some common sense guidelines are that tests and long papers usually count more than other types of work and should receive a higher grade weight. Quizzes and homework assignments are often equally weighted. In #2 below, we use a grade weight distribution of Tests = 2, Quizzes = 1, and Lessons = 1. (The following example calculations use the **Science** information from the Grading Chart on the previous page.)

Formula 1
A. Total of all % scores per type of work = _____
B. Total # of scores (grades) per type of work = _____
C. Percent grade for type of work = A/B = _____
D. Grade Weight: _____

Example: Type of work = **Science Lessons**
A. Total of all % scores per type of work = <u>524%</u>
B. Total # of scores (grades) per type of work = <u>6</u>
C. Percent grade for type of work = A/B = <u>87.3%</u>
D. Grade Weight: <u>1</u>

SCIENCE DATA		
Using the information from the Grading Chart on the previous page and **Formula 1**		
Type of Work	**Percent Grade**	**Grade Weight**
Lessons	87.3%	1
Quizzes	89.3%	1
Tests	93.3%	2

2. To determine the **FINAL GRADE** for each individual subject, use **Formula 2** below:

Formula 2
$$\frac{(\text{Percent grade for type of work} \times \text{Grade weight}) + (\text{Percent grade for type of work} \times \text{Grade Weight}) + \text{etc.}}{\text{Total all Grade Weights}}$$

For **Science** the final grade is calculated using **Formula 2** and the **SCIENCE DATA** above. The final percentage is *rounded to the 'ones' position. Then a final grade is assigned from **TABLE 1** (below) as follows:

$$\frac{(87.3 \times 1) + (89.3 \times 1) + (93.3 \times 2)}{1 + 1 + 2} = 90.8\% \text{ round to } \mathbf{91\%} \qquad \mathbf{FINAL\ GRADE = A-}$$

3. The following tables are to be used to determine grades. **TABLE 1** is a straight grading table. **TABLE 1** is best used for most routine subjects and to encourage your student to improve his/her educational skills. **TABLE 2** is a curved grading table. **TABLE 2** should be used sparingly with extremely difficult to master subjects or challenges.

TABLE 1

A+	97-100%	C-	70-72%
A	93-96%	D+	67-69%
A-	90-92%	D	63-66%
B+	87-89%	D-	60-62%
B	83-86%	F+	57-59%
B-	80-82%	F	53-56%
C+	77-79%	F-	50-52%
C	73-76%		

TABLE 2

A+	93-100%	C-	67-69%
A	90-92%	D+	63-66%
A-	87-89%	D	60-62%
B+	83-86%	D-	57-59%
B	80-82%	F+	53-56%
B-	77-79%	F	50-52%
C+	73-76%	F-	47-49%
C	70-72%		

SECTION C

Two types of report cards are provided at the end of this planner. The **top** report card is a **letter evaluation** report card for the elementary grades where a letter grade is not required (Grades K-3 or K-6). The **bottom** report card is a **letter graded** report card equivalent to state and federal reporting requirements for higher grades. Use it when a grade is required or needed to assess student progress and skills (Grades 4-12 or 7-12).

Fill in the blanks of the report card, you will use, by typing or printing in the appropriate information. Remember to include the name of each subject studied. Assignment of a letter value for the top report card is subjective and should be approached with prayer and comparison of effort and mastery to the subject presented and studied. For the bottom report card write the **FINAL GRADE** for the whole subject as determined in **SECTION B #2** above.

***How to round**: 0.5-0.9 round up; 0.1-0.4 round down. Examples: 81.5-81.9% round to 82%; 81.1-81.4% round to 81%.

SEMESTER: 1

SAMPLE OF HOW TO TALLY AND GRADE

JUNE/BOB GRADE 9
Student/Grade Level
Science
Subject

Final Grade
A-
Grading Table
1

LESSONS
Type of work

# of Grades (**A**)		% (**1**)		# of Grades (**B**)		% (**2**)		# of Grades (**C**)		% (**3**)	
A+		x100=		C+		x79=		F+		x59=	
A	II	x95=	190	C	I	x75=	75	F		x55=	
A-	I	x92=	92	C-		x72=		F-		x52=	
B+		x89=		D+		x69=		Totals:			
B	I	x85=	85	D		x65=		%Totals : **1+2+3**			524
B-	I	x82=	82	D-		x62=		# Grades: **A+B+C**			6
Totals: 5			449	Totals: 1			75	%Grade= %Totals / # Grades		4	87.3%
								GRADE WEIGHT		**D**	1

QUIZZES
Type of work

# of Grades (**A**)		% (**1**)		# of Grades (**B**)		% (**2**)		# of Grades (**C**)		% (**3**)	
A+		x100=		C+		x79=		F+		x59=	
A	II	x95=	190	C		x75=		F		x55=	
A-		x92=		C-		x72=		F-		x52=	
B+		x89=		D+		x69=		Totals:			
B	I	x85=	85	D		x65=		%Totals : **1+2+3**			357
B-	I	x82=	82	D-		x62=		# Grades: **A+B+C**			4
Totals: 4			357	Totals: 0			0	%Grade= %Totals / # Grades		5	89.3%
								GRADE WEIGHT		**E**	1

TESTS
Type of work

# of Grades (**A**)		% (**1**)		# of Grades (**B**)		% (**2**)		# of Grades (**C**)		% (**3**)	
A+	I	x100=	100	C+		x79=		F+		x59=	
A	I	x95=	95	C		x75=		F		x55=	
A-		x92=		C-		x72=		F-		x52=	
B+		x89=		D+		x69=		Totals:			
B	I	x85=	85	D		x65=		%Totals : **1+2+3**			280
B-		x82=		D-		x62=		# Grades: **A+B+C**			3
Totals: 3			280	Totals: 0			0	%Grade= %Totals / # Grades		6	93.3%
								GRADE WEIGHT		**F**	2

RAW GRADE: $\frac{[(4 \times D)+(5 \times E)+(6 \times F)]}{(D+E+F)}$

$\frac{(87.3 \times 1) + (89.3 \times 1) + (93.3 \times 2)}{1+1+2}$
= 90.8% rounded to 91%

Final Grade = Round raw grade to two digit percentage, then apply grade.

SEMESTER: _____

_____
Student/Grade Level

_____
Subject

Final Grade
Grading Table

_____
Type of work

# of Grades (**A**)	% (**1**)	# of Grades (**B**)	% (**2**)	# of Grades (**C**)	% (**3**)
A+	x100=	C+	x79=	F+	x59=
A	x95=	C	x75=	F	x55=
A-	x92=	C-	x72=	F-	x52=
B+	x89=	D+	x69=	Totals:	
B	x85=	D	x65=	%Totals : **1+2+3**	
B-	x82=	D-	x62=	# Grades: **A+B+C**	
Totals :		Totals:		%Grade= %Totals / # Grades	4
				GRADE WEIGHT	**D**

Type of work

# of Grades (**A**)	% (**1**)	# of Grades (**B**)	% (**2**)	# of Grades (**C**)	% (**3**)
A+	x100=	C+	x79=	F+	x59=
A	x95=	C	x75=	F	x55=
A-	x92=	C-	x72=	F-	x52=
B+	x89=	D+	x69=	Totals:	
B	x85=	D	x65=	%Totals : **1+2+3**	
B-	x82=	D-	x62=	# Grades: **A+B+C**	
Totals :		Totals:		%Grade= %Totals / # Grades	5
				GRADE WEIGHT	**E**

Type of work

# of Grades (**A**)	% (**1**)	# of Grades (**B**)	% (**2**)	# of Grades (**C**)	% (**3**)
A+	x100=	C+	x79=	F+	x59=
A	x95=	C	x75=	F	x55=
A-	x92=	C-	x72=	F-	x52=
B+	x89=	D+	x69=	Totals:	
B	x85=	D	x65=	%Totals : **1+2+3**	
B-	x82=	D-	x62=	# Grades: **A+B+C**	
Totals:		Totals:		%Grade= %Totals / # Grades	6
				GRADE WEIGHT	**F**

RAW GRADE: [(4xD)+(5xE)+(6xF)]
            (D+E+F)

Final Grade = Round raw grade to two digit percentage, then apply grade.

DAILY GRADES-_____

SUBJECT   STUDENT

DAILY GRADES-_____

SUBJECT STUDENT

SUBJECT STUDENT

DAILY GRADES-_____

SUBJECT

STUDENT

SUBJECT

DAILY GRADES- _____
SUBJECT   **STUDENT**

DAILY GRADES-_____
SUBJECT   STUDENT

DAILY GRADES-_____
SUBJECT   STUDENT

REPORT CARD

_____
SCHOOL NAME

PRINCIPAL:_____

GRADE:　　　　**YEAR:**　　　　**SEMESTER:**
STUDENT:　　　　　　　**TEACHER:**

O-OUTSTANDING　　　　**F**-FAILURE
G-GOOD　　　　　　　　**I**-INCOMPLETE
S-SATISFACTORY　　　　**P**-PASSED
BA-BELOW AVERAGE　　　**NP**-NOT PASSED

SUBJECT	GRADE	SUBJECT	GRADE

REPORT CARD

_____
SCHOOL NAME

PRINCIPAL:_____

GRADE:　　　　**YEAR:**　　　　**SEMESTER:**
STUDENT:　　　　　　　**TEACHER:**

A-OUTSTANDING　　　　**F**-FAILURE
B-GOOD　　　　　　　　**I**-INCOMPLETE
C-SATISFACTORY　　　　**P**-PASSED
D-BELOW AVERAGE　　　**NP**-NOT PASSED

SUBJECT	GRADE	SUBJECT	GRADE

This page reproducible for purchaser's use only, not for any other purpose nor for distributions to any other person, group, or organization.

AN APPOINTED TIME FOR CHANGE

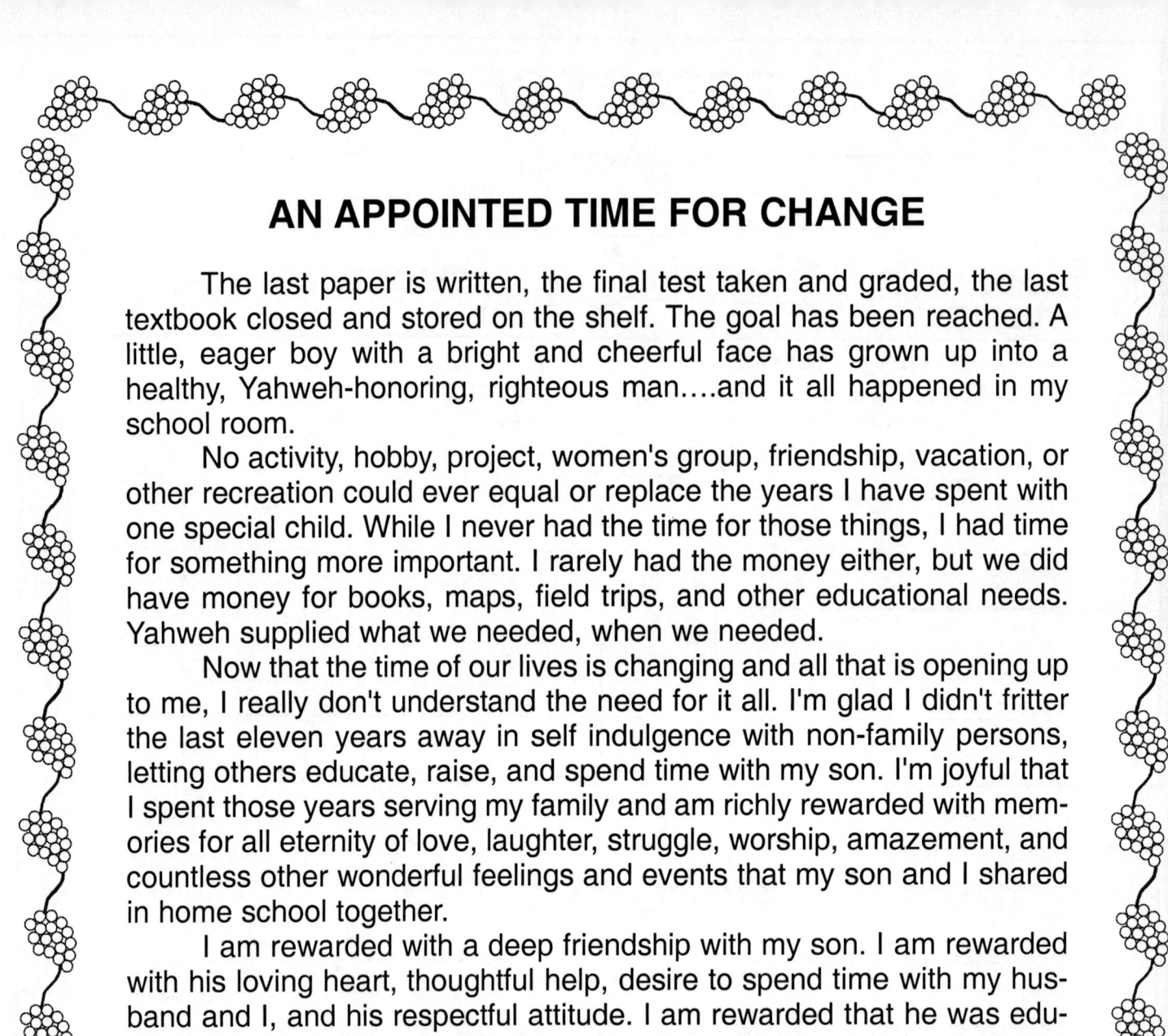

The last paper is written, the final test taken and graded, the last textbook closed and stored on the shelf. The goal has been reached. A little, eager boy with a bright and cheerful face has grown up into a healthy, Yahweh-honoring, righteous man....and it all happened in my school room.

No activity, hobby, project, women's group, friendship, vacation, or other recreation could ever equal or replace the years I have spent with one special child. While I never had the time for those things, I had time for something more important. I rarely had the money either, but we did have money for books, maps, field trips, and other educational needs. Yahweh supplied what we needed, when we needed.

Now that the time of our lives is changing and all that is opening up to me, I really don't understand the need for it all. I'm glad I didn't fritter the last eleven years away in self indulgence with non-family persons, letting others educate, raise, and spend time with my son. I'm joyful that I spent those years serving my family and am richly rewarded with memories for all eternity of love, laughter, struggle, worship, amazement, and countless other wonderful feelings and events that my son and I shared in home school together.

I am rewarded with a deep friendship with my son. I am rewarded with his loving heart, thoughtful help, desire to spend time with my husband and I, and his respectful attitude. I am rewarded that he was educated well and will enter his first year of college as a sophomore at a good Christian college....Yes, the time of life is changing. School is over for both of us, but everything has had a reason and purpose under Ya, for we have sought His will and set our hearts to follow no matter how hard or easy the path was.

For every matter there is an appointed time,
even a time for every pursuit under the heavens.
Qoheleth/Ecclesiastes 3:1

Special thanks to:
Kimberley Nash

PREPARING A TRANSCRIPT

A transcript may be required anytime a student is applying to an institution of higher education or transferring from home school to a public or private school. Preparing a transcript is not hard, it just takes a little work. If you have been diligent about grading, preparing, and keeping report cards, you will be able to find most of the information you need for your transcript with ease. To begin you must understand the terminology used to prepare a transcript. The following definitions will help you.

Units: the number of points assigned to a subject. This is usually assigned by the number of hours per week a student spends in class/study for a particular subject.

One unit is equal to **three** hours per week,
Two units are equal to **six** hours per week,
Three units are equal to **nine** hours per week,
Four units are equal to **twelve** hours per week,

Grade: the letter grade earned at the completion of a class subject: A, A-, B+, B, B-, C+, C, C-, D+, D, D-, F.
Grade points: the number of points assigned to each grade, as show in this chart.

GRADE	GRADE POINTS	GRADE	GRADE POINTS
A	4.00	C	2.00
A-	3.67	C-	1.67
B+	3.33	D+	1.33
B	3.00	D	1.00
B-	2.67	D-	0.67
C+	2.33	F	0.00

Attempt: the total number of units attempted for a particular semester or quarter.
Earn: the number of units completed for a particular semester or quarter.
Pass: the number of units completed successfully for a particular semester or quarter that are not assigned a grade.
Quality: the number of units attempted minus the number of units passed for a particular semester or quarter.
Points: the number of units times the grade points earned, via the grade, for a subject that has been completed for a particular semester or quarter.
GPA: grade point average is the number of points divided by the quality.
Ses/Quar: these are abbreviations for the words semester and quarter, respectively.
Cum: the cumulative numbers to date for each category.

The following shows how to prepare a transcript for one semester and cumulatively between more than one semesters.

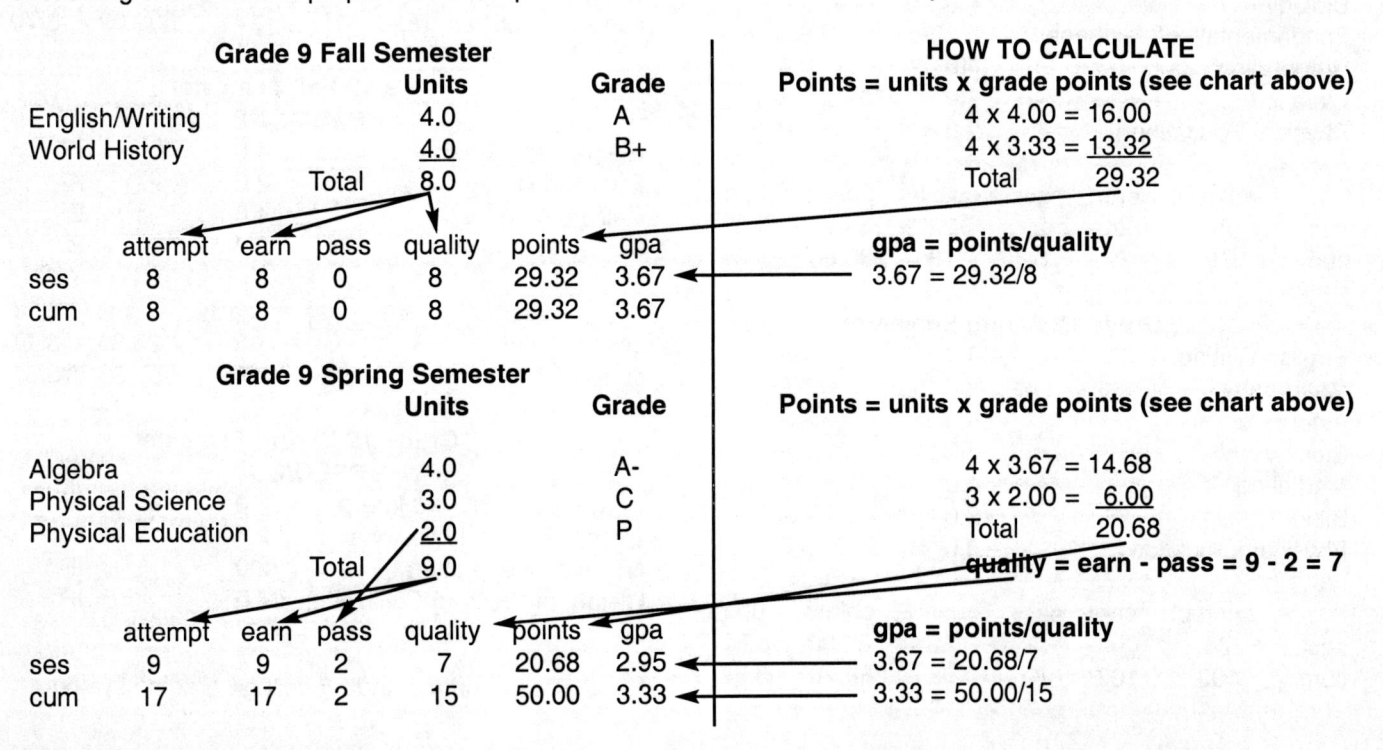

Grade 9 Fall Semester

	Units	Grade
English/Writing	4.0	A
World History	4.0	B+
Total	8.0	

HOW TO CALCULATE
Points = units x grade points (see chart above)
4 x 4.00 = 16.00
4 x 3.33 = 13.32
Total   29.32

	attempt	earn	pass	quality	points	gpa
ses	8	8	0	8	29.32	3.67
cum	8	8	0	8	29.32	3.67

gpa = points/quality
3.67 = 29.32/8

Grade 9 Spring Semester

	Units	Grade
Algebra	4.0	A-
Physical Science	3.0	C
Physical Education	2.0	P
Total	9.0	

Points = units x grade points (see chart above)
4 x 3.67 = 14.68
3 x 2.00 = 6.00
Total   20.68

~~quality~~ = earn - pass = 9 - 2 = 7

	attempt	earn	pass	quality	points	gpa
ses	9	9	2	7	20.68	2.95
cum	17	17	2	15	50.00	3.33

gpa = points/quality
3.67 = 20.68/7
3.33 = 50.00/15

RESURRECTION ACADEMY
1250 Central Street
Alabaster, TX 35123

HOME SCHOOL
OFFICIAL TRANSCRIPT

Cynthia Alissa Jones

Graduation Date: 5-28-05

June 1, 2005

Grade 9 Fall Semester

Course	Credits	Grade
English/Writing	4.0	A
French 2	4.0	A
World History	4.0	B+
Algebra	4.0	B+
Physical Science	4.0	B+
Bible	2.0	A
Physical Education	2.0	A

	attempt	earn	pass	quality	points	gpa
ses	24	24	0	24	87.96	3.67
cum	24	24	0	24	87.96	3.67

Grade 9 Spring Semester

Course	Credits	Grade
English/Writing	4.0	A
French 2	4.0	A
World History	4.0	A
Algebra	4.0	A
Physical Science	4.0	A
Computer Graphic Design	4.0	A
Family Management	3.0	A
Bible	2.0	P
Physical Education	2.0	P

	attempt	earn	pass	quality	points	gpa
ses	31	31	4	27	108.00	4.0
cum	55	55	4	51	195.96	3.84

Grade 10 Fall Semester

Course	Credits	Grade
English/Writing	4.0	A-
Geography	4.0	A
Algebra 2	4.0	A-
Biology	4.0	A
Fundamentals of Textbook Preparation	4.0	A
Bible	2.0	A-
Physical Education	2.0	P

	attempt	earn	pass	quality	points	gpa
ses	24	24	2	22	84.70	3.85
cum	79	79	6	73	280.66	3.85

Grade 10 Spring Semester

Course	Credits	Grade
English/Writing	4.0	A
Geography	4.0	A-
Algebra 2	4.0	A-
Biology	4.0	A-
Marketing	4.0	A
Bible	2.0	A
Physical Education	2.0	P

	attempt	earn	pass	quality	points	gpa
ses	24	24	2	22	84.04	3.82
cum	103	103	8	95	364.70	3.84

Grade 11 Fall Semester

Course	Credits	Grade
English/Writing	4.0	B+
US History/Government	4.0	A-
Advanced Math	4.0	A
Chemistry	4.0	A-
Personnel Management	3.0	A-
Health	3.0	A
Physical Education	2.0	P

	attempt	earn	pass	quality	points	gpa
ses	24	24	2	22	81.69	3.71
cum	127	127	10	117	446.39	3.82

Grade 11 Spring Semester

Course	Credits	Grade
US History/Government	4.0	B
Advanced Math/Business Math	4.0	B+
Chemistry	4.0	A-

	attempt	earn	pass	quality	points	gpa
ses	12	12	0	12	40.00	3.33
cum	139	139	10	129	486.39	3.77

PSEO

Course	Credits	Grade
History of Ancient Israel	4.0	B+
Basic Computer Applications	1.0	P
Fitness	1.0	A
Concepts of Astronomy	3.0	A
Concepts of Astronomy Lab	0.0	S
Foundations of Communication	3.0	C+
Elementary Greek I	4.0	C+

	attempt	earn	pass	quality	points	gpa
ses	16	16	1	15	45.63	3.042
cum	155	155	11	144	532.02	3.70

Grade 12 Fall Semester
PSEO/CDE

Course	Credits	Grade
Elementary Greek II	4.0	IP
Christian Discipleship	2.0	A-
College Algebra	4.0	B
Introduction to Music	2.0	B

	attempt	earn	pass	quality	points	gpa
ses	12	8	0	8	25.34	3.17
cum	167	163	11	152	557.36	3.67

Grade 12 Spring Semester
PSEO/CDE

Course	Credits	Grade
Principles of Biblical Interp	2.0	IP
Evangelism and Missions	2.0	IP
NT History and Literature	2.0	IP
History of Western Civilization	4.0	IP

Based on a standard college grading system.

THE FRUIT OF PERSEVERANCE

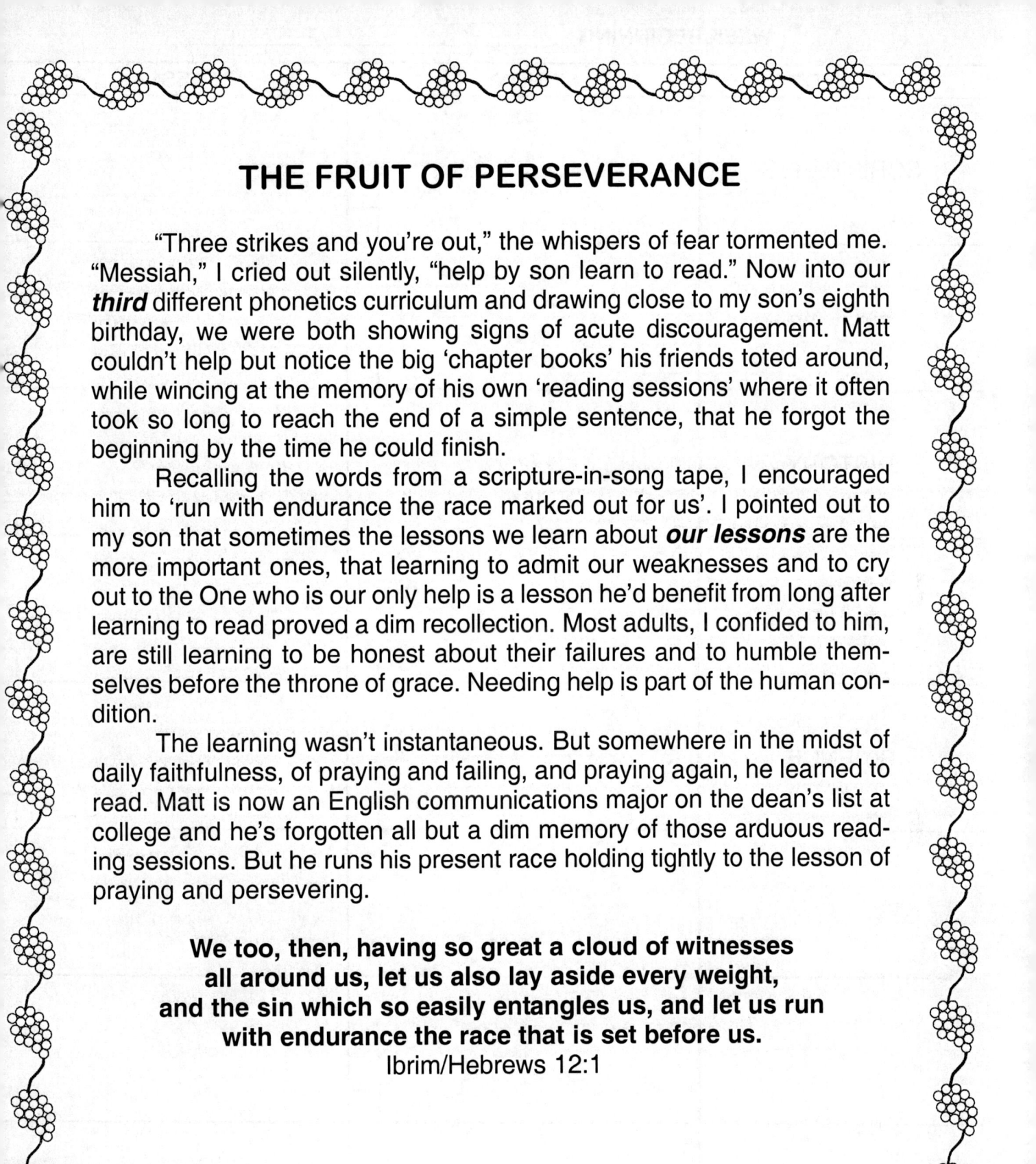

"Three strikes and you're out," the whispers of fear tormented me. "Messiah," I cried out silently, "help by son learn to read." Now into our *third* different phonetics curriculum and drawing close to my son's eighth birthday, we were both showing signs of acute discouragement. Matt couldn't help but notice the big 'chapter books' his friends toted around, while wincing at the memory of his own 'reading sessions' where it often took so long to reach the end of a simple sentence, that he forgot the beginning by the time he could finish.

Recalling the words from a scripture-in-song tape, I encouraged him to 'run with endurance the race marked out for us'. I pointed out to my son that sometimes the lessons we learn about **our lessons** are the more important ones, that learning to admit our weaknesses and to cry out to the One who is our only help is a lesson he'd benefit from long after learning to read proved a dim recollection. Most adults, I confided to him, are still learning to be honest about their failures and to humble themselves before the throne of grace. Needing help is part of the human condition.

The learning wasn't instantaneous. But somewhere in the midst of daily faithfulness, of praying and failing, and praying again, he learned to read. Matt is now an English communications major on the dean's list at college and he's forgotten all but a dim memory of those arduous reading sessions. But he runs his present race holding tightly to the lesson of praying and persevering.

**We too, then, having so great a cloud of witnesses
all around us, let us also lay aside every weight,
and the sin which so easily entangles us, and let us run
with endurance the race that is set before us.**
Ibrim/Hebrews 12:1

Special thanks to:
Susan Zelie

WEEK BEGINNING _____

SUBJECT	MONDAY	TUESDAY
SCRIPTURES		
ENGLISH		
HISTORY		
MATH		
SCIENCE		
NOTES		

WEDNESDAY	THURSDAY	FRIDAY

WEEK BEGINNING_____

SUBJECT	MONDAY	TUESDAY
SCRIPTURES		
ENGLISH		
HISTORY		
MATH		
SCIENCE		
NOTES		

WEDNESDAY	THURSDAY	FRIDAY

WEEK BEGINNING_____

SUBJECT	MONDAY	TUESDAY
SCRIPTURES		
ENGLISH		
HISTORY		
MATH		
SCIENCE		
NOTES		

WEDNESDAY	THURSDAY	FRIDAY

WEEK BEGINNING _____

SUBJECT	MONDAY	TUESDAY
SCRIPTURES		
ENGLISH		
HISTORY		
MATH		
SCIENCE		
NOTES		

WEDNESDAY	THURSDAY	FRIDAY

WEEK BEGINNING _____

SUBJECT	MONDAY	TUESDAY
SCRIPTURES		
ENGLISH		
HISTORY		
MATH		
SCIENCE		
NOTES		

WEDNESDAY	THURSDAY	FRIDAY

WEEK BEGINNING_____

SUBJECT	MONDAY	TUESDAY
SCRIPTURES		
ENGLISH		
HISTORY		
MATH		
SCIENCE		
NOTES		

WEDNESDAY	THURSDAY	FRIDAY

WEEK BEGINNING_____

SUBJECT	MONDAY	TUESDAY
SCRIPTURES		
ENGLISH		
HISTORY		
MATH		
SCIENCE		
NOTES		

| WEDNESDAY | THURSDAY | FRIDAY |

WEEK BEGINNING_____

SUBJECT	MONDAY	TUESDAY
SCRIPTURES		
ENGLISH		
HISTORY		
MATH		
SCIENCE		
NOTES		

WEDNESDAY	THURSDAY	FRIDAY

WEEK BEGINNING_____

SUBJECT	MONDAY	TUESDAY
SCRIPTURES		
ENGLISH		
HISTORY		
MATH		
SCIENCE		
NOTES		

WEDNESDAY	THURSDAY	FRIDAY

WEEK BEGINNING_____

SUBJECT	MONDAY	TUESDAY
SCRIPTURES		
ENGLISH		
HISTORY		
MATH		
SCIENCE		
NOTES		

WEDNESDAY	THURSDAY	FRIDAY

WEEK BEGINNING_____

SUBJECT	MONDAY	TUESDAY
SCRIPTURES		
ENGLISH		
HISTORY		
MATH		
SCIENCE		
NOTES		

WEDNESDAY	THURSDAY	FRIDAY

WEEK BEGINNING _____

SUBJECT	MONDAY	TUESDAY
SCRIPTURES		
ENGLISH		
HISTORY		
MATH		
SCIENCE		
NOTES		

WEDNESDAY	THURSDAY	FRIDAY

WEEK BEGINNING _____

SUBJECT	MONDAY	TUESDAY
SCRIPTURES		
ENGLISH		
HISTORY		
MATH		
SCIENCE		
NOTES		

WEDNESDAY	THURSDAY	FRIDAY

WEEK BEGINNING_____

SUBJECT	MONDAY	TUESDAY
SCRIPTURES		
ENGLISH		
HISTORY		
MATH		
SCIENCE		
NOTES		

WEDNESDAY	THURSDAY	FRIDAY

WEEK BEGINNING _____

SUBJECT	MONDAY	TUESDAY
SCRIPTURES		
ENGLISH		
HISTORY		
MATH		
SCIENCE		
NOTES		

WEDNESDAY	THURSDAY	FRIDAY

WEEK BEGINNING_____

SUBJECT	MONDAY	TUESDAY
SCRIPTURES		
ENGLISH		
HISTORY		
MATH		
SCIENCE		
NOTES		

WEDNESDAY	THURSDAY	FRIDAY

WEEK BEGINNING _____

SUBJECT	MONDAY	TUESDAY
SCRIPTURES		
ENGLISH		
HISTORY		
MATH		
SCIENCE		
NOTES		

WEDNESDAY	THURSDAY	FRIDAY

WEEK BEGINNING_____

SUBJECT	MONDAY	TUESDAY
SCRIPTURES		
ENGLISH		
HISTORY		
MATH		
SCIENCE		
NOTES		

WEDNESDAY	THURSDAY	FRIDAY

WEEK BEGINNING_____

SUBJECT	MONDAY	TUESDAY
SCRIPTURES		
ENGLISH		
HISTORY		
MATH		
SCIENCE		
NOTES		

WEDNESDAY	THURSDAY	FRIDAY

WEEK BEGINNING_____

SUBJECT	MONDAY	TUESDAY
SCRIPTURES		
ENGLISH		
HISTORY		
MATH		
SCIENCE		
NOTES		

WEDNESDAY	THURSDAY	FRIDAY

WEEK BEGINNING_____

SUBJECT	MONDAY	TUESDAY
SCRIPTURES		
ENGLISH		
HISTORY		
MATH		
SCIENCE		
NOTES		

WEDNESDAY	THURSDAY	FRIDAY

WEEK BEGINNING_____

SUBJECT	MONDAY	TUESDAY
SCRIPTURES		
ENGLISH		
HISTORY		
MATH		
SCIENCE		
NOTES		

WEDNESDAY	THURSDAY	FRIDAY

WEEK BEGINNING _____

SUBJECT	MONDAY	TUESDAY
SCRIPTURES		
ENGLISH		
HISTORY		
MATH		
SCIENCE		
NOTES		

WEDNESDAY	THURSDAY	FRIDAY

WEEK BEGINNING _____

SUBJECT	MONDAY	TUESDAY
SCRIPTURES		
ENGLISH		
HISTORY		
MATH		
SCIENCE		
NOTES		

WEDNESDAY	THURSDAY	FRIDAY

WEEK BEGINNING _____

SUBJECT	MONDAY	TUESDAY
SCRIPTURES		
ENGLISH		
HISTORY		
MATH		
SCIENCE		
NOTES		

WEDNESDAY	THURSDAY	FRIDAY

WEEK BEGINNING _____

SUBJECT	MONDAY	TUESDAY
SCRIPTURES		
ENGLISH		
HISTORY		
MATH		
SCIENCE		
NOTES		

WEDNESDAY	THURSDAY	FRIDAY

WEEK BEGINNING_____

SUBJECT	MONDAY	TUESDAY
SCRIPTURES		
ENGLISH		
HISTORY		
MATH		
SCIENCE		
NOTES		

WEDNESDAY	THURSDAY	FRIDAY

WEEK BEGINNING _____

SUBJECT	MONDAY	TUESDAY
SCRIPTURES		
ENGLISH		
HISTORY		
MATH		
SCIENCE		
NOTES		

WEDNESDAY	THURSDAY	FRIDAY

WEEK BEGINNING _____

SUBJECT	MONDAY	TUESDAY
SCRIPTURES		
ENGLISH		
HISTORY		
MATH		
SCIENCE		
NOTES		

WEDNESDAY	THURSDAY	FRIDAY

WEEK BEGINNING _____

SUBJECT	MONDAY	TUESDAY
SCRIPTURES		
ENGLISH		
HISTORY		
MATH		
SCIENCE		
NOTES		

WEDNESDAY	THURSDAY	FRIDAY

WEEK BEGINNING _____

SUBJECT	MONDAY	TUESDAY
SCRIPTURES		
ENGLISH		
HISTORY		
MATH		
SCIENCE		
NOTES		

| WEDNESDAY | THURSDAY | FRIDAY |

WEEK BEGINNING _____

SUBJECT	MONDAY	TUESDAY
SCRIPTURES		
ENGLISH		
HISTORY		
MATH		
SCIENCE		
NOTES		

WEDNESDAY	THURSDAY	FRIDAY

WEEK BEGINNING_____

SUBJECT	MONDAY	TUESDAY
SCRIPTURES		
ENGLISH		
HISTORY		
MATH		
SCIENCE		
NOTES		

WEDNESDAY	THURSDAY	FRIDAY

WEEK BEGINNING_____

SUBJECT	MONDAY	TUESDAY
SCRIPTURES		
ENGLISH		
HISTORY		
MATH		
SCIENCE		
NOTES		

| WEDNESDAY | THURSDAY | FRIDAY |

WEEK BEGINNING_____

SUBJECT	MONDAY	TUESDAY
SCRIPTURES		
ENGLISH		
HISTORY		
MATH		
SCIENCE		
NOTES		

WEDNESDAY	THURSDAY	FRIDAY

WEEK BEGINNING _____

SUBJECT	MONDAY	TUESDAY
SCRIPTURES		
ENGLISH		
HISTORY		
MATH		
SCIENCE		
NOTES		

| WEDNESDAY | THURSDAY | FRIDAY |

RESURRECTION RESOURCES PRODUCTS

BIBLE

HISTORY OF THE BIBLE

SCRIPTURES

HISTORY

THE SIGNERS
OF THE DECLARATION OF INDEPENDENCE

WORLD HISTORY-SPAIN

WORLD HISTORY-THE NETHERLANDS

ENGLISH

CREATIVE WRITING

HOW TO WRITE BOOK REPORTS

ENGLISH AND WRITING: GRADE 8

HOW TO WRITE ESSAYS AND RESEARCH REPORTS: LEVEL A

HOW TO WRITE ESSAYS AND RESEARCH REPORTS: LEVEL B

LITERATURE AND WRITING:
GRADE 9/LEVEL ONE

WORLD HISTORY REPORT WRITING:
NETHERLANDS
SPAIN

MATH

MATH: KINDERGARTEN

SCIENCE

HOW TO WRITE LAB REPORTS

LAB EQUIPMENT

LAB KITS

MORE LAB REPORTS: LEVEL ONE

MORE LAB REPORTS: LEVEL TWO

SCIENCE: GRADE 7

SCIENCE: GRADE 8

THE PERIODIC TABLE OF THE ELEMENTS

SCHOOL SUPPLIES

ART PACKS

HOME SCHOOL DAILY PLANNER

ERASERS

PENCILS

TO RECEIVE A CATALOG OR ORDER ANY OF THESE PRODUCTS
CONTACT:
RESURRECTION RESOURCES
www.thefathersbooks.com
1-651-578-1581